LET'S LOOK AT BIRDS

Written and illustrated by
Wendy Meadway

Language consultant
Diana Bentley
University of Reading

The Bookwright Press
New York • 1990

Let's Look At

Aircraft
Bears
Big Cats
Bicycles and Motorcycles
Birds
Castles
Circuses
Colors

Dinosaurs
Farming
Horses
Monster Machines
Outer Space
Racing Cars
Rain
The Seasons

Sharks
Ships and Boats
Sunshine
Tractors
Trains
Trucks
Volcanoes
Whales

First published in the
United States in 1990 by
The Bookwright Press
387 Park Avenue South
New York, NY 10016

First published in 1990 by
Wayland (Publishers) Ltd
61 Western Road, Hove
East Sussex BN3 1JD, England

© Copyright 1990 Wayland (Publishers) Ltd

Library of Congress Cataloging-in-Publication Data
Meadway, Wendy.
   Let's look at birds/by Wendy Meadway.
      p. cm. – (Let's look at)
   Includes bibliographical references (p.
   ISBN 0–531–18340–8
   1. Birds—Juvenile literature.   I. Title.
   II. Series: Let's look at (New York, N.Y.)
   QL676.2.M43   1990
   598—dc20   89–18221
                                                   CIP

Phototypeset by Kalligraphics Ltd, Horley, Surrey
Printed by Casterman, S.A., Belgium

Words printed in
bold are explained
in the glossary

Contents

The first birds

Long ago, before birds existed, **dinosaurs** lived on the Earth. Some of them were quite small and looked a little like lizards. Gradually, over millions of years, these dinosaurs became covered with feathers. At the same time, their front legs became wings, which enabled them to fly. These were the first birds.

The first flying bird was called Archaeopteryx (say *Ar-kee-op-ter-ix*). Probably it only used its wings to **glide** from tree to tree.

All the birds we see today have warm blood. Their babies are born inside eggs. Most birds can fly – but not all of them!

How birds fly

Birds have strong **muscles** joining the wings to the **breastbone**. The wings have big feathers at the ends. As the bird flaps its wings, these feathers help to drive it through the air. Birds use their tail feathers for steering and braking.

Wing feathers

Body feathers

Birds are light enough to fly because many of their bones are hollow. They have small, soft feathers on their bodies. The feathers give them a smooth surface, which helps them to travel through the air more easily.

Bird shapes

Birds come in many different shapes and sizes. The shape of a bird depends on its **habitat** or the food that it eats. Some birds have big wings for gliding. Others have long legs for walking in shallow water.

Splendid wren

Lily-trotter

Flamingo

Many birds that perch in trees have special muscles for holding onto branches. Some birds with very long toes can walk on floating leaves.

The shape of the beak depends on whether the bird uses it to snap up insects, catch fish or crack open nuts and fruit.

Paradise flycatcher

Toucan

Little owl

Keeping clean

Birds must keep their feathers clean so that they can fly properly. Sometimes they bathe in water. You can watch a bird sitting on a branch and shaking itself after bathing. It then **preens** its feathers by pulling them through its beak.

Cardinal bathing

Lovebirds preening

Some birds use dust to bathe in. This cleans their feathers and gets rid of **parasites**. Jays have a very clever way of getting rid of their parasites. They pick up ants and put them under their feathers. This is called anting. The ants squirt out an **acid** that drives the parasites away.

Jay anting

Sparrows dust-bathing

Finding a mate

Male birds try to find a female **mate**. The male sings loudly to warn other males not to enter his **territory**. He tries to attract a female by showing off. This is called courtship.

Grebes

Peacock

Peacocks show off by spreading out their enormous fans of brightly colored feathers. Cranes leap around as if they were dancing. Male and female grebes show off to each other by preening, shaking their heads and dancing around in the water.

Cranes

Building a nest

Birds lay eggs from which their chicks **hatch**. Eggs can be eaten by other animals, so the parent birds try to protect them. They build nests or lay their eggs in safe places, such as inside hollow trees.

House martin

Weaver bird

Chaffinch

There are many different types of
nests. They may be made of twigs,
leaves, pieces of mud or clay.
Weaver birds build nests by
weaving grasses together.
Hummingbirds make little cuplike
nests from moss. Guillemots lay
eggs on cliff ledges. The eggs are
shaped so that they do not roll off!

Woodpecker

Guillemot

Hummingbird

Puffins

A puffin's nest is very unusual. Puffins live in **burrows** under the ground – just like rabbits! During the **breeding season** their beaks become large and colorful. This is why they are often called "parrots of the sea."

A puffin spends all its life on cliffs or at sea, feeding on small eels and other fish. It can carry a lot of food in its big beak. Here you can see a puffin in its burrow in a cliff.

Sea birds

Some birds catch fish from the sea to eat. They dive into the water and swim after the fish. Here you can see a cormorant swimming underwater chasing a fish.

Gannets

Cormorants

Pelicans

Pelicans have big beaks with a large pouch of skin underneath. They use the pouch like a net to scoop up fish from the sea.

Gannets have long arrow-like bodies. They dive into the sea from high in the sky.

Flightless birds

Some birds have such weak or small wings that they cannot fly. The ostrich has very soft **plumage** instead of stiff feathers in its wings and tail. It uses its strong legs to run away from enemies.

Kiwis cannot fly because their wings are so small. In fact, they look as though they have no wings at all! Kiwis are found only in New Zealand.

Kiwi

Ostriches

20

Penguins live mainly in
Antarctica, near the South Pole.
They cannot fly but they are very
good swimmers. They use their
wings as flippers.

Penguins

21

Parrots

Most parrots come from **tropical** countries. People like to keep them as pets because they have very colorful plumage. Some parrots can copy noises. They sound as though they are talking!

There are hundreds of different kinds of parrots. Every parrot has a big hooked beak that is strong enough to crack open hard nuts. Parrots have strong feet with four toes. Two toes point forward and two point backward.

Water birds

Many birds live by rivers, lakes or ponds. Most of these birds get their food from the water. Ducks eat insects and underwater plants. Herons catch fish in their beaks. Geese, though, **graze** on the grassy banks beside rivers or ponds.

Heron

Mallard (male)

Great northern diver

Mallard (female)

Swan

Many water birds have broad, flat bodies for floating on the water and **webbed feet**, which they use as paddles. They have long necks for reaching food under the water.

Canada goose

Great northern
diver

Birds of prey

Some birds eat small animals for food. They have strong hooked beaks, sharp claws and very good eyesight for hunting and catching their **prey**.

Birds of prey can be very small, like the tiny falconets, or very big, like eagles. Some eagles have wings that are 10 feet (3 m) across.

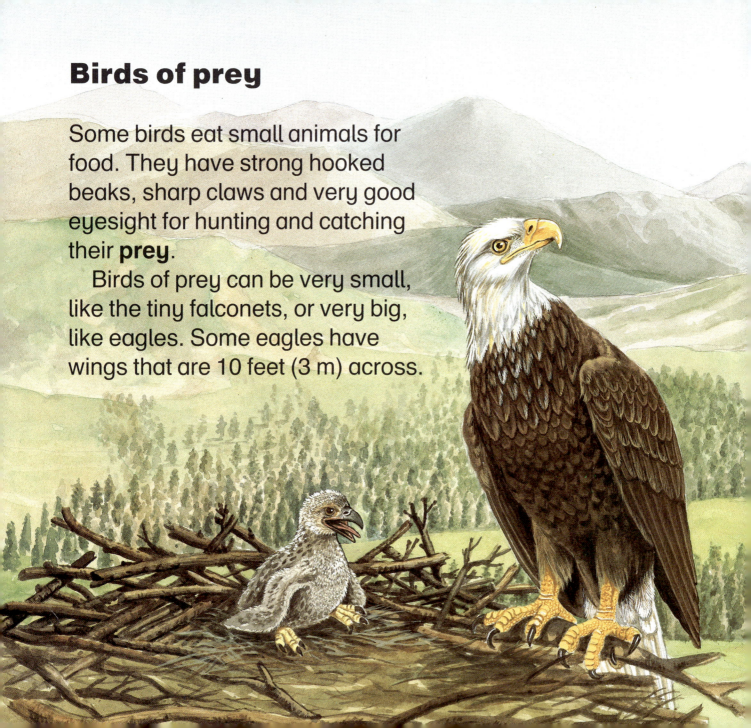

Some birds of prey are now quite **rare**. On the left is the rare bald eagle, which is found in the United States, and below is a golden eagle.

Backyard birds

Most of the wild birds you see near houses once lived in the woods. They moved into gardens and yards where there was more food.

These birds eat seeds, berries, and even orchard fruit! They also help gardeners because they eat harmful insects.

Sparrow

Collared doves

You can encourage birds to come to your yard by putting up a bird feeder with bread or seeds on it or by hanging up a bag of peanuts.

Blackbird

Robin

Chaffinch

Blue tit

Glossary

Acid A liquid that tastes sour and can burn your skin.

Breastbone The long flat bone in the bird's chest.

Breeding season The time of year when birds join together to produce their chicks.

Burrow A hole in the ground that an animal lives in.

Dinosaurs Animals that lived on Earth long ago.

Glide To move smoothly through the air without flapping the wings.

Graze To eat grass.

Habitat The area where an animal normally lives.

Hatch To break out of an egg.

Mate One of a pair of animals that joins together to produce young.

Muscles The parts inside the body attached to the bones. Muscles tighten or become loose in order to make the body move.

Parasites Animals that live and feed on other animals.

Plumage A bird's feathers.

Preen   To clean and
   arrange the feathers.
Prey   An animal that is
   hunted by another animal
   for food.
Rare   Very few in number.
Territory   A nesting or
   hunting area that one pair
   of birds will defend against
   other birds.
Tropical   From the very
   hot parts of Africa, South
   America, Asia and
   Australia.
Webbed feet   Feet that
   have toes joined together
   by skin.

Books to read

Birds by Carolyn Boulton
   (Franklin Watts, 1984)
Birds of Prey by Kate Petty
   (Gloucester, 1987)
*Discovering Ducks, Geese, and
   Swans* by Anthony Wharton
   (Bookwright, 1987)
Discovering Sea Birds by Anthony
   Wharton (Bookwright, 1987)
Life Cycle of a Duck by Jill Bailey
   (Bookwright, 1988)
Life Cycle of an Owl by Jill Bailey
   (Bookwright, 1989)
The Penguin by Angela Royston
   (Warwick, 1988)

Index